Business process automation with

BPMS

Business process automation with BPMS

Ingénierie des Processus•net
Concevoir l'Organisation

http://www.ingenieriedesprocessus.net

The author has taken care in the preparation of this book, but makes no expressed or implied warranty of any kind and assumes no responsibility for errors or omissions. No liability is assumed for incidental or consequential damages in connection with or arising out of the use of the information contained herein.

Comments and feedback are welcome. They may be addressed directly to the author's website.

First edition

ISBN 978-1-326-07420-3

Copyright © 2014 Briol Patrice

Patrice
Briol

Business process automation with

BPMS

Also by Patrice Briol

- BPMS L'automatisation des processus métiers
- BPMN 2.0 Distilled
- Les Fondements de l'Architecture d'Entreprise
- Ingénierie des processus métiers, de l'élaboration à l'exploitation
- BPMN, the Business Process Modeling Notation, Pocket Handbook
- XML, le langage des systèmes de gestion des processus métiers
- PalmOS Programmation, Applications professionnelles en C et Java (Dunod)

Contents

Preface 7

Introduction 11

Part I Business Process Management 15

    The task 16

    Business processes and automation 18

    From BPM to BPMS 20

Part II The origin of the Automation 27

    Specialization 28

    Mass production limits 29

    A systematized labor division 31

    Assembly line production 33

    Managing the production 35

    When it goes wrong 37

    The human relations movement 39

    The social consequences of automation 43

    Systems and systems thinking 54

- Organizational configurations 61
- Bureaucracy 67
- Machine bureaucracy 68
- Professional bureaucracy 69
- Contingency factors 69
- Technology and organization 72
- Variability controlled by formalizing 75
- Power and control 75
- Parkinson law 80
- Neo-Taylorism 81
- Energy and organization 84
- The organization life cycle 87
- Organizational silos 89
- Outsourcing 93

Part III Business Process Automation 99
- Automate business processes 100
- BPMS implementation 108
- Consequences 117

Conclusion 123

Preface

Is this book yet another discussion of business process management implementation matter? The answer is not really. My first business process management book published in 2008 focused on the implementation of a continuous company's improvement life cycle from defining strategic objectives to solutions implementation. Among those solutions, it introduced the technical ability to automate business processes with a dedicated system, or the BPMS. Subsequently, technologies have evolved and currently the latter offers widely new features to translate easier the theoretical business processes models into executable ones. That progress has significantly reduced the gap between the model and its execution within its reality.

Managers have also found their interests within the newly proposed means, like the real-time monitoring of their enterprise process execution. Despite those technical enhancements, many companies seem reluctant to endorse the Business Process Management (BPM) approach to sustain their business. They generally limit its acceptance to the documentation of their business processes or more simply to just provide their operational procedures. Therefore, the process optimization or organizational improvements are limited to the submission of some recommendations to the management at the operational level processing.

In this book, the terms *enterprise* or *company* refer to any establishments producing an *intangible* output including nonprofit organizations. Their *immaterial* production considers the information as a raw material like the one used within an industrial production, which produces, by default, a tangible outcome. Thus, doing business for the former means to load, transform, store, and distribute information through its business processes performance. Consequently, how is it possible to create a link between the machines' introduction from the industrialization age and the automation of the business process supported by the Business Process Management System (BPMS)? This book aims to answer that question by describing the origins and the consequences of the automation principles in the heavy industry applied to the current business process. That approach raises a second question during its automation implementation phase: is the *mechanistic* perception of the company enough to be able to implement the BPMS easily? Unfortunately not, as that perception has to be completed with the concepts and principles depicted by the sociology of organizations in order to take care on the human aspects within the enterprise.

This book combines selected information from the literatures on that subject, completed by my own experience in the BPM and BPMS field. It assists the reader to find a line of thought between the different paths currently exposed in this book within three main parts:

- The first part introduces the principles of business process management and its automation approach, which is usually introduced by the main BPM's market players. This book remains on the basic concepts without going deep into the underlying technical details.
- The second part describes the automation origins and its evolution through various concepts and principles that emerged over the years. It also introduces the principles of the enterprise's sociological theory as the

foundation used to explain the organization structure and its way to operate their business.
- The last part links the relevant aspects and consequences of the industrial revolution with the contemporary BPM approach in order to identify some potential issues of the BPMS implementation.

In conclusion, this book attempts to determine the most appropriate environment and its prerequisites for a successful BPMS implementation by following the main principles of the immaterial production automation.

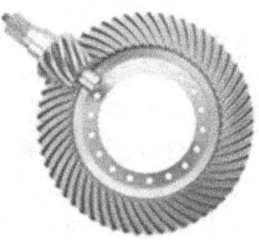

Introduction

In recent years, Business Process Management (BPM) has become a benchmark for holistic management and enterprise's business processes improvement. That approach intends primarily three major goals for the company:

- Customers' satisfaction
- Improved performance
- Cost reduction

In fact, that approach combines some activities already practiced for a long time in existing business management:

- Business processes analysis and optimization
- Operational management
- Process automation
- Business processes documentation, modeling and mapping
- Corporate governance

Business Process Management System greatly simplifies the automation of the business processes.

That dedicated information system centralizes all business interactions. It also introduces many user-friendly tools to design easily the executable process models, to define several ways of information publishing and sharing or define the key performance indicators used for the real-time processes execution monitoring.

Despite this, many companies are reluctant to follow that way as reported by an independent European Office's survey on French companies' usages and practices. That report[1] has revealed some interesting issues:

- The vast majority of companies' managers endorse the BPM approach in their company
- Lack of internal skills hinders the overall BPM projects' success
- Many users like the processes automation, but few Chief Information Officers (CIO) are opting to automate them. Following that study, only 6 percent of the surveyed enterprises automate parts of their business processes
- The BPM approach will often be limited to business processes description with models
- In many cases, BPM is limited to laconic models, which are described with relatively

---

[1] "Le CXP — La gestion des processus métier en France – Enquête 2013 sur les usages et les pratiques des entreprises françaises (2013)"

- inadequate office tools, even in the case of complex process representation needs
- Few major BPMS implementation projects succeed
- Often, management ignores such a project's return on investment (ROI) and understates the control of the gap between the original objectives and effective results
- The processes covered by automation are primarily those showing numerous interactions with the centralized corporate information. The latter is also operating within a large collaborative dimension system
- The BPMS implementation initially covers the administrative activities followed later by the integration of a higher benefit business process matching

Following that study, we can say that the BPM approach receives the management support as long as its implementation scope is limited to the graphical formalization done with office tools. Indeed, that method simply answers the minimalist business processes information centralization need without systematically measuring its appropriateness. Such definition reduces the BPM and BPMS scope to the maintenance of a single enterprise information repository, while the BPMS offers more benefits to the company and allows it to achieve the three major objectives previously defined.

Let us go back to the description of the Business Process Management initiative and its goals.

Part I
Business Process Management

The task

Under the proposed Webster's definition, a task is *a labor or study imposed by another, often in a definite quantity or amount*. In case of project management matter, the Wikipedia encyclopedia defines a task as the one *to be accomplished within a defined period of time or by a deadline*. However, the French definition of the task includes a price in return of its execution. Therefore, by mixing all of those definitions and for our point of interest, the definition should be *the responsibility taking in the performance of an activity pursuing a specific purpose, producing an expected outcome against resource consumption within a defined period of time*.

The *goal* aims to lead the decision-making or enforce the action. Without a predefined goal set, the task performance remains arbitrary.

There are two categories of tasks:

- The *manual* task performed by a human
- The *automated* task performed by an automaton or a mechanism, possibly assisted by the human

The optimization of the task execution is determined to reach the goal and produces the expected result:

- Within a *minimum execution delay* with a theoretical value equal or close to zero
- Within a *minimum resources usage* with a theoretical value equal or close to zero

The process optimization is reached when those criteria values remains constants through all successive repetitions of activities performance. Measures deviations usually represent the first indication of seeking business process improvement.

Activity is a combination of unordered tasks unlike a *process*, which contains logically, ordered tasks. An industrial production often combines two types of activities:

- The *administrative* activity related to the management and the control of the production environment. Its tasks are indirectly involved in the production process.
- The *operational* activity directly implied within the goods and services production processes.

In a comprehensive approach, a business process may include both categories, but this is not always the case. Depending on the business activity, *administrative business processes* include exclusively the administrative tasks entirely dissociated from the production's ones.

Business processes and automation

A business process corresponds to the logical and successive tasks execution, which produce a predefined outcome. Each produced outcome at the intermediate task execution constitutes the final product. In the same way, the total process resources consumption should be logically equal to the sum of intermediaries' resources consumption. However, that logic is not valid in the real world: the business processes' execution requires a minimum coordination setup. Coordination effort is itself a task that also consumes its own resources. Therefore, the final product includes also indirectly the implied coordination effort. The organizations' goals often forgot that effort event if without them the production remains almost impossible.

Based on these assumptions, a business process optimization will follow some axioms:

- Maximizing production inputs usage as far as optimizing the tasks performance
- Maximizing the reduction of the administrative tasks and resources intake

There are two major ways in order to optimize the enterprise efficiency:

- The *classical* approach drives the optimization changes directly within the organizational

structure: improving jobs, working conditions, defining or redefining the hierarchical structure functions, controls, and so forth. This approach usually takes the form of injunctions addressed to the line managers.
- The *automation* introduces robots and mechanisms to replace manual tasks in order to enable the whole production to be free from human intervention.

Automation appeared during the industrial revolution of the nineteenth century. Meeting the time expectations, automation pursued the increasing of productivity goals, reducing production costs and therefore:

- Increasing margins
- Increasing production rates
- Reducing defects with the production of standardized products
- Reducing some crafts difficulties
- Reducing low benefit and repetitive tasks

Automation has enabled the transition from handcraft production into the industrial age while raising the overall wealth level. *Industrialization* means: standardized products mass production that releases humans from tedious and repetitive tasks. While it is relatively easy to visualize nowadays automation in the primary and secondary sectors, such as mining and raw materials processing, that visualization exercise is much-less convenient for the tertiary sector. A so-called *intangible* outcome such as consulting, insurance, banking, training, education and research, administration, or personal services combine the administrative and coordination tasks within their production processes. Therefore, for them, the *immaterial production* corresponds to the information processing. Indeed, automation in such cases looks like the computer processing implementation. The information processing within the production of services outcomes corresponds to the handling of raw material in industrial production.

Optimizing an intangible production process relies on the automation of the information processing by adding the following objectives to the main efficiency optimization objectives:

- Improve information gathering, transportation, and storage
- Improve information treatments
- Improve information exchange in various formats on several communication channels

From BPM to BPMS

The Business Process Management is a comprehensive approach to align business processes with their clients' expectations and needs. That systematic method aims to improve the company's efficiency and effectiveness continuously by integrating innovation, flexibility, and technology. That definition appears to be THE solution to any problems encountered in the company's production process. Within a continuous improvement cycle, the company would be able to answer quickly to its customer's expectations while easily integrating changes and environmental constraints. That approach considers the enterprise under the idea of *mechanistic* approach: the enterprise works perfectly under the deterministic consideration where the BPM's approach implementation follows a defined life cycle as described by the Deming principles:

- *Plan* or set the objectives to achieve. In BPM's perspectives, set the measurable goals in order to improve the company's business processes
- *Do* or develop and implement improvement solution
- *Check* by comparing obtained measurements following up the implementation and the expected values fixed earlier
- *Act* or adjust the design following the shift observed in the previous step

The life-cycle implementation applied to the BPM approach may requests more sub-activities:

- Analyze the situation as the measurements basis
- Model the current or *As-Is* situation
- Determine the improvement needs based on Key Performance Indicators (KPI)
- Assess potential improvement solutions
- Model the foreseen improved *To-Be* situation
- Simulate complex situations
- Design solutions and new tools that should improve the situation
- Build and implement the organizational structure and the new production process
- Deploy the finalized *To-Be* processes
- Execute the new processes
- Measure the gaps
- Analyze measures
- Improve the situation
- Check the differences between results and initial objectives

The BPM approach implementation often seems easily applied within the manufacturing industry based on standardized products production than within the service sector and its intangible production outcome. As mentioned earlier, organizational framework change and task automation support the overall business processes optimization initiative. The objective will focus much about production tasks automation than the administrative ones. In this case, the automated information processing may take two distinctive forms:

- A *primary* form characterized by a complex heterogeneous information systems accumulation revolving around a centralized one. Some perceptive users develop and add in the business their own office applications. Email exchanges and shared folders are mainly used to exchange information among business processes' stakeholders. Originally, users developed their own solutions in order to facilitate their daily work in response to the possible difficulty with the CIO to answer all IT requests. These adjuncts generally supported the administrative activities such as labor distribution between team members or used as an activity reports generation and delivery to the hierarchy level.
- An *advanced* form characterized by the control of all information exchanges and sequential tasks execution among the stakeholders in accordance with the business processes logic definition. This way of working integrates existing systems and formalizes exchanges in order to monitor changes throughout the process' activities performance. In such cases, that *workflow* system also manages the labor distribution and

control along several predefined parameters set.

The BPMS addresses this second fully automated processing information form. That system adds some functionality to the original workflow engine. Therefore, it contains at least four main components:

- The process engine offers the process modeling and execution
- The management and analytical reports generation from collected information allowing users to identify weaknesses, trends, and opportunities in order to react quickly to the current situation
- The content management system addresses information and documents storage issues
- The collaboration tool eases the information exchange between the stakeholders, the resources, and the tasks allocation

From the users' point of view, the BPMS collaborates with them within electronic input forms displayed on their electronic devices. They insert the related business information or attach existing office documents within the displayed form. Once they have validated their inputs, the system acquires and handles those data following the predefined business logic sequence[2]. The BPMS may also offer the possibility to automate information handled with predefined algorithms. Finally, it integrates the existing systems by allowing the information exchange within the complete IT architecture through various channels.

From the managers' point of view, the BPMS appears to be a dashboards' reporting system based on the measurements taken in real-time directly from the production environment. That feature allows them to bring rapidly and effectively adequate answer to various encountered situations.

The BPM approach and its BPMS implementation seems to answer the question of continuous operational improvement following the Cartesian logic. Indeed, it appears relevant to automatize the business process to simplify the enterprise's organization and way of working perception as a mechanism did it. Then, the perception of the organization looks like a perfect mechanism answering in a coherent and consistent manner to all internal or external solicitations. However, that Cartesian approach responds only partially to the automation needs as noticed from the main report result on BPMS's implementation. In general, the enterprise considers the BPMS like any other piece of software and delegates its

---

[2] Nowadays, major BPMS vendors use the BPMN standard notation to represents that business logic workflows.

implementation to the IT department. Usually, that implementation fails from the lack of consideration for the comprehensive approach suggested by the BPM approach. The BPMS implementation's activity would reduce or even neglect the potential impacts on the organizational aspects.

Following the organizational sociology history, the human behavior showed significant changes when it faces working-way fluctuations in a dedicated environment. However, the BPMS introduces in the company substantial changes in the way of working, including the autonomy level as a significant risk issue for the implementation project success.

The past studies in the organization and automation fields bring a special perspective in order to define favorable conditions driving the BPMS deployment success. Let us go back to the origins of the automation, its causes, and consequences to try to define if similarities may appear nowadays.

Part II
The origin of the Automation

Specialization

The task distribution to achieve a goal is not a new paradigm. Sharing work among people occurred since before antiquity as evidenced by the paintings and other hieroglyphics dating back to those distant times. However, its study and formalization is relatively new in the perspectives of history.

There are two ways to assign tasks to individuals:

- Each individual performs every production stage to realize the outcome.
- Individuals perform tasks based on their skills. From the labor division or specialization point of view, the individual controls only his or her activities and not the entire production. Individuals collectively produce the expected outcome. The coordination effort level is significantly higher than the first way described above.

In 1776, the Scotsman Adam Smith[3] was the first economist that formalized the labor division principles, its performance, and its consequences through its implementation within an English factory. An increasingly specialized production process division

---

[3] "Life of Adam Smith", John Rae, 1895
"An Inquiry into the Nature and Causes of the Wealth of Nations", Adam Smith, 1776

accompanies the labor division. This specialization increases the operators' efficiency and productivity effects, and thus, increases the standardized products production. For Smith, specialization promotes the exchange between producers and consumers leading the entire population's happiness within the liberal thinking of that time.

However, Smith also discusses the effects of the specialization limitations applied to many workers and the oversupply risk in a market restricted by the lack of consumers. He noticed also that the labor division pushed to its maximum led to a disastrous effect on the workers' minds that are brutalize by repetitive tasks requiring them always to make the same motions. In this case, the operator autonomy and its decision-making disappear. Therefore, the balance between the repetitive work allocation and the operator's autonomy limits the labor division principle.

Mass production limits

In 1858, the neoclassical producer theory[4] suggests an economic behavioral model based on *economic agents* as goods and services producer[5]. Agents are perfectly rational and totally informed. They transform inputs I into outcome O within a production function f. The company looks like a "black box" performing its

---

[4] Walras, Jevons, Pigou, Pareto, etc.
[5] "Principles of Economics", Carl Menger, 2011

production function in a market characterized by a pure and perfect competition. According to this hypothesis, the production function supports the calculation of the maximum amount that the producer can expect to achieve given the consumed inputs quantity. Economists, or the so-called "marginalism" behind this theory, conclude that the yield change, which is equivalent to the marginal return, decreases when production inputs increase.

The production inputs encompass three main categories:

- Work
- Natural resources
- Capital

Therefore, the producer focuses on maximizing the combined benefit to minimizing production costs leading to equilibrium between the production level and the optimized input consumption. Beyond that, each additional unit of output is more expensive than the previous with decreasing marginal returns. Indeed, the increase in production provides the means for the company to spread its fixed costs and reduce the unit cost in response to economies of scale. However, from a production level, the average fixed cost reduction decreases and the unit cost eventually increases with the return attenuation. The minimum marginal unit cost inflection point becomes the producer's goal.

This discussion naturally leads to include automation in the production in order to replace repetitive work as long as the capital investment is lower than the expected production gains.

A systematized labor division

The process result is composed by the outcomes of its intermediate tasks. Each worker receives some goals and means to achieve those intermediate results. Business processes optimization would correspond to optimal labor division according to the best distribution of the workers competencies.

In 1911, Taylor published his Scientific Management principles[6] as the systematic labor division approach based on two topics:

- The *horizontal* division down the production process into simple tasks series assigned to a specialized operator. The engineer identifies the most-effective method to split the work between operators. This effectiveness research is based on the scientific approach by using various means:

---

[6] "The Principles of Scientific Management", Frederick Winslow Taylor, 1997

- - o Measuring each elementary movement delay
  - o Eliminating unnecessary time
  - o Searching for the most suitable tools to execute tasks
  - o Defining an optimum for each production time stage
  - o Drafting the procedures
- The *vertical* division distinguishing work design and training tasks on the one hand and on the other hand the implementation tasks. For Taylor, the engineer defines exclusively the activities and working conditions while the operators simply execute the tasks.

Taylorism seeks to standardize the task execution without systematically pursuing to automate and standardize an entire production. The approach [7] is preferably focused on the quest for the "one best way" to perform the task. A rigorous methods and techniques obtained with a detailed analysis drives to an optimal production definition. However, its implementation consequences are noticeable with the work dehumanization marked by large amounts of absenteeism and later with the birth of social conflicts within the enterprise. That principle defines a production system by considering the human as

---

[7] "The One Best Way: Frederick Winslow Taylor and the Enigma of Efficiency", Robert Kanigel, 2005

machine achieving its highly predictable task without any autonomy. In conclusion, the tasks specialization is limited by the minimal required level of autonomy for the worker. The workstation automation level will put off so far that limit of worker's autonomy.

Taylorism hardly supports the intellectually complex work or the activities characterized by a lack of standardization.

Assembly line production

In 1908, Ford includes the Taylor's scientific management principles in the production of his cars: each skilled worker operates on a specific car's component. Each worker performs his activity and completes the result produced by routing to the next working station. The vehicle assembly takes place at a particular location with its components coming with each delivery. In order to improve further the productivity, Ford created the assembly line production. The workers restrict their movements on their workstation. Bands continuously carry the parts needed for each worker and its outcome moves through the line. The car moves along the assembly line and it is gradually completed with its parts. The assembly line has reduced the elapsed time to build the car from six hours to less than one hour and a half.

These results have generated much interest in the industrial world and the idea became a doctrine[8] based on several axioms:

- Vertical and horizontal work division within the organization helps to define the production-line implementation.
- The standardized series mass production based on interchangeable parts.
- The operators participate in productivity by giving them the financial access to their outcomes. This availability is done with low-cost goods production. That approach increases the consumption, which supports also the production.

The use of supply chain and automation gradually replacing the manual tasks and routing documents confirms the increase of the standard outcome production productivity. The worker becomes an element of the production. Now, the automated production line sets the worker's pace of intervention.

Like Taylor, and Smith before him, Ford observed operators' pronounced disinterest in repetitive tasks. This behavior occurs very rapidly with the dropouts' onset and a significant workers turnover frequency.

---

[8] "Between Fordism and Flexibility: The Automobile Industry and Its Workers", Johnathan Zeitlin and Stephen Tolliday, 1992

To remedy this[9], Ford increases workers' wages by passing them to $5 an hour when at the same time a Ford-T model costs $300. The mass production of a standardized product lowers the business margin. To keep the same benefits, the enterprise has to sell larger volumes[10].

Ford addresses some social problems bluntly: he joined a private militia to reprimand any social movement such as strikes and banned labor unions within the company. He also introduced spies in assembly lines to identify agitators and protesters.

The application of Fordism in a company can only be conceived by the appearance of a mass consumption of its largely standardized product.

Managing the production

In 1916, Henri Fayol focuses on the operator management by establishing the first production management tracks and particularly the modern management concepts rationalization and formalization[11]. It suggests the presence of five functions in business:

---

[9] Ford has a significant low-skilled workers volume primarily stemming from immigration of that time.
[10] Between 1908 and 1927, Ford produced fifteen million of the Ford-T.
[11] "General and Industrial Management", Henri Fayol and Constance Storrs, 2013

- *Technical* to produce, process, and manufacture
- *Commercial* to buy, sell, and trade
- *Financial* to research and optimum capital usage
- *Security* for persons and property protection
- *Accountant* to payroll calculation, assets, and wealth census statistics

He supplements this list by adding the transverse administration function with five key activities (POCCC)

- Plan
- Organize
- Command
- Coordinate
- Check or Control

In his study, he also suggested the establishment of dedicated administration tools. By identifying information from production, it becomes possible for the supervisor to respond quickly and directly on the production line in order to correct deviations. Administrative tasks increase the production costs. However, they remain necessary to ensure smooth production running.

In his book, Fayol identifies some key management elements:

- Crafty labor division
- Authority and responsibility
- Discipline
- Command unit with a multi-level hierarchy
- Individual interests subordination to the general interest
- Compensation and participation in the company's results
- Information and decisions centralization
- Order
- Equity
- Stability
- Initiative
- Union staff

Productivity requires a systematic monitoring of administrative tasks that are essential for the production. Management becomes "involved" in production, always aiming to improve business productivity.

When it goes wrong

Considering the enterprise as a "black box" machine maintains the idea that the workers take the appearance of its working gears. That machinery within a fully controlled environment dominates the early-twentieth-century industrial view of the production. From the assembly line, working conditions degrade quickly. An uncontrolled goods production and lack of consumers cause social disorder and outbreaks. This mechanism eventually stops as the first strikes broke out.

In the 1930s, Merton [12] studied the effects and the consequences of social disorder. He based his working on the Durkheim (1893) research [13]. Previously designated as the *anomie*, the social disorder appears from the failure to comply with some basic social rules:

- Respect for cultural purposes in regard to the company members' wishes and expectations
- The rules prescribing the means proposed to stakeholders in order to achieve their own goal
- The available resources distribution among stakeholders

The established social norms regulate the humans' conduct and ensure them a social order. The disintegration of those norms reveals the anomie. To be more precise, anomie weakens the close relationship between the goals and the available means to achieve those. On the contrary, a strong cohesion between goals and means ensures the social peace within the organization. A thoughtless industrialization focused

---

[12] "Social Theory and Social Structure", Robert K. Merton, 1968
[13] "Suicide: A Study In Sociology", Emile Durkheim, George Simpson, John Spaulding, 1997

only on short-term company's revenues will create anomie by missing the respects of individuals' goals since they disappear from the top management's view. The top management often accentuates that anomie by defining overall objectives that are not easily translatable at the operational levels of the company.

The human relations movement

The principles of working division and their consequences in its implementation represent the worrying issues in the quest for the overall company's performance. In early 1929, the American economic growth slows following a sharp increase from the 1920s. A thought movement was born in the 1930s with the emergence of the Human Relations Movement School. That new thinking focuses on human beings in response to the failures observed within the Taylorist approach. That approach tries to answer some questions about the dehumanization of working conditions and its consequences:

- Ensure worker's job rotations. The workers occupy various workstations to avoid routine and disinterest. In the same way, they will give a global overview of the overall production while before they are limited to a real restricted view of that production.

- Reduce fragmented, arduous and repetitive tasks in order to improve the intervention level on allocated tasks.
- Broaden the work intervention scope to other tasks, such as machinery adjusting or maintenance involving a greater degree of the worker's responsibility.
- Increase the worker's autonomy. Let the possibility for the workers to organize their work to reach a production level or objectives set by the management.
- Set up *quality circles* with voluntary workers that come together in order to improve the production process and product quality. This initiative calls into question the vertical Taylor's labor division in which only the head determines the quality level. The finished products' quality level definition involves henceforth directly the workers.

Driven by Elton Mayo [14], the Human Relations Movement takes place with the identification of several principles observed in various American's companies:

- Financial remuneration is not the lone motivator. It just completes the means of

---

[14] "The Human Problems of an Industrial Civilization", Elton Mayo, 2003

motivation and other key happiness sources may appear in the eyes of the worker.
- The tasks division is not effective in all areas.
- Reintroduce the notion of a group for the worker with the meaning for them to belonging to it. This initiative helps to give back the human being position to the center of work and its social reality.
- Allow the employee an intellectual autonomy level that he can at best enjoy the job, and finally restore some individual power.

On the contrary to the principle of *"produce more to earn more"*, the Human Relations Movement experiences increases the individual's interest without changing anything in their environment and tends to improve productivity. This sudden incentive led workers to excel in their jobs. However, this improvement would remain temporary and limited to the individual level. Over the time, these effects will disappear. The production's performance will tend to the weakest one observed among the group's members.

Moreover, the meaning of the *group*, hitherto ignored with Taylorism and Fordism approaches, takes a significant level in the Mayo's analysis. The group life existence revolved around tensions and general moral directly influences the whole productivity. As viewed like a social system, the group redefines the roles and responsibilities of each. Now, the new paradigm involves that the supervisor listens and deals instead of practicing strict and one-way authority.

The Human Relations Movement has many branches with dozen of authors. Each of them brings its idea and improves commonly the movement. The following table summarizes some of these principles and its complemented management tools.

	Mayo	Herzberg[15]	Mc Gregor[16]
Principles	Promote informal relationships and bring interest to employees	Generate satisfaction by changing the hygiene factors and motivation	Converge individual goals and company objectives
Tools	- Establish working groups - Empower - Develop internal communication - Fostering a democratic management way	- Meeting hygiene - Create a framework ergonomic - Premiums, awards, broader tasks, work and responsibilities	Enhance both parties interests by taking shares in the company or in the stock options form

---

[15] "The Motivation to Work", Frederick Herzberg, Bernard Mausner, Barbara Bloch Snyderman, 1993
[16] "The Human Side of Enterprise", Douglas McGregor, 2006

Moreover, the Human Relations Movement will become later the theoretical foundation for most human resources management applied in enterprises.

The social consequences of automation

Since the early twentieth century, people share their work with machines pursuing the same objective of productivity improvement. Eventually, those machines have substantially contributed to improve the overall company efficiency. With the development of advanced technology and despite the Human Relations Movement principles implementation, some questions about the human role within the industrial production remain uncertain.

The sociology has spawned into several specialized disciplines after the Second World War. The sociology of organization studies how actors build and coordinate the organized activities within entities called *organizations*. In 1958, many sociologists [17] have written some comments on the social consequences of the automation within the industry[18].

In 1958, there were three ways to define *automation*:

---

[17] Crozier, Freidmann, Naville, Enzig, Diebold, Morse or Gass.
[18] International Bulletin of Social Sciences, "the social consequences of automation", 1958

- The continuous production line, which integrates many automated tasks and runs without any manual interventions.
- The introduction of feedback devices, which adjust automatically the production line output with the expected results. These mechanisms reduce the gap between the objectives and the measures of the reality. Finally, they increase the products output quality.
- The integration of computers, which mainly support the administrative tasks.

Within the Fordism, the assembly lines include both workers and semi-automated devices. By definition, the automation aims to replace completely the human interventions with transfer and tools machines. The thinking behind the automation is to convert easily the indefinitely repeated actions, which require few professional skills, into mechanized tasks.

The remaining non-automated tasks on the assembly line employ some workers. For the latter, the role and the utility of their actions or their intermediate results may appear as not to be so significant or eventually without intrinsic interest. In the production-line paradigm, the machine dictates the pace of work to individuals. This imposed measure represents a major cause of unhappiness in workers. Machines know neither fatigue, nor disease, nor contesting support on repetitive tasks. However, this new assignment may complicate the technology usage within the assembly line.

The pace of work and the complexity are not the sole consequences:

- Jobs occupied by skilled workers decrease.
- Both the transfer machines and devices feedback reduces checkpoints.
- The significant increase of preparation and maintenance tasks requesting naturally skilled individuals. The new maintenance specialist has more knowledge and less experience than the former repair worker.
- Work becomes less independent. They fit in close to those of engineers and engineering office relations.
- Once the routine tasks are automated, the operator can take responsibility for the whole operations cycle.

Given these consequences, automation extends beyond the sole new technology introduction in the production perimeter. Automation also incorporates a methodological framework as a way to rethink the production organization as a whole. Depending on the production unit size, automation may cause considerable changes and workforces displacement.

This depends also on the conditions of the labor replacement, which vary greatly from one company to another.

For the operator, the first impression of automation appears to be a very sensitive working and safety conditions improvement. However, several fundamental questions appear to the worker following the automation:

- He has some specialized skills and knowledge. What about the depreciation risk of those?
- What will be the work and new working conditions after the implementation project?
- Is there still a work for him within the enterprise? Could automation lead him out of work?

According to Rosenberg, the great defect of automated units leads more or less to the downfall of curiosity among the workers. Alternatively, replacing operators by automate reinforces this finding. Operators do not work anymore directly on such matters. They do it through signals with lights or symbols. The operator's view of the production becomes more theoretical because of the process virtualization. So, operators cease to be interested in automated stations since the latter represent nothing real and, then, it is no longer necessary to have questions to ask about it. When the operator has to move itself to a new job, two kinds of problems may arise for him: new skills acquisition and the content of that job.

These issues carry for the operator a series of fears and generally larger concerns regarding the acquisition of new skills in real life. The automation requires a precise coordination of tasks. This tends to increase further the operator responsibility. Peoples' anxiety increases if the newly allocated tasks have possibly more severe consequences for them than before. In consequences, production's error levels may also rise in such cases. An operator may encounter some difficulties to execute a new task if the latter is too complex or too abstract for him. The skills depreciation represents an anxiety source even more important than the unemployment fear for the operator. The idea that automation can significantly alter the skills generates this anxiety state. This finding is especially significant when the company has to retrain its operators and that operation appears to be too expensive for the company and very difficult to evolve for the operator.

George Friedman, in his submissions, has also highlighted the human problems associated with industrial mechanization, from the physiological line-work effects to the vocational skills and job satisfaction issues. He has found that the increase of measurement instruments requires operators to react very often to visual and auditory signals. While semi-automatic machines involve the physical fatigue of the operator, automation creates a perceptual fatigue. In commercial operations, the feedback often calls for the human agent intervention to correct the situation and realize the expected goal. The operator must now stand on their toes, doing nothing specific: he or she should only be prepared to act quickly in case of failure in the manufacturing process. A new anxiety factor has emerged, characterized by a lively attention with a passive mobility.

Automation introduces complex systems within the production, which substitutes manual tasks previously reserved for the expert operators' hands. The technical complexity tends to give more benefit to the academic theoretical education than the learning and doing *on the way*. Automation introduces a shift in employment from the operator to the tool maintenance.

- The activity of the maintenance operator who was partially responsible for the machine tools maintenance is becoming increasingly important while their counterparts who working directly on production lines eventually disappear. After the automation implementation on production, the maintenance operator replaces the former responsible to the maintenance of the workstation machine tool. Following Naville's ideas, maintenance operators incorporate the operation control and thus involve the rapid rehabilitation activity. That new activity requires more flexibility and varied skills than ever before. This is why the move of the former operators has raised some difficulties, mainly because the pace of work now depends on some technical factors, some new working conditions, and specific skills.

- Automation increases productivity with automated operations efficiency, but it also increases the operators' skills. Following that logic, operators should therefore see their incomes increase in line with the acquisition of new responsibilities. Formerly to the automation, the pay system had linked the operator salary and its work amount. A high salary corresponds to a large production volume. Automation breaks that individual relationship with the labor volume. Performance and results become collective. Increased efficiency tends to increase wages. This is also due to the production chain former operators' shift to that maintenance requiring more skills. Dissociation between compensation and production volume results in the collective performance calculation instead of individual performance clashing with the individual qualities' differentiation extent. To remedy this, the company adds therefore the liability premiums weighted according to the responsibility level.

- Automation denotes also a source of fear for operators, such as losing their job. Following the sociologists' opinions, this figure may vary depending on the economic environment in which automation operates. The automation implementation realized during a growth period limits the effect on unemployment. The enterprise tries to prevent the workers to join the competition due to the labor surplus made because of automation. Conversely, the automation increase in a negative growth period also raises the unemployment figures. Tight margins and vast labor availability at low cost trigger the start of a job destruction cycle. Both considerations show us the importance of the implementation period choice. The elapsed time between the project planning and its real implementation within the production environment affects significantly the timing choice. Automation achieved in crisis times would follow an economic logic that the enterprise performs results at the best during the recovery time.

Poor timing means that the opposite will happen. In this regard, the unions had noted in 1958 that companies left behind in the race to automation suffered the most thereafter, and were much less advanced than those companies that made the change earlier.

- Following the Naville's study, the automation of the production line does not increase directly the supervisory staff, nor its management or administrative departments. However, automation may affect the hierarchy in searching to preserve their position.
- Automation requests the company and its operators some substantial changes not only in how to act, but also in the way to think about its production. For a company and its management, adopting successfully advanced automation technologies ask them to agree to change deeply the methods in their mindset. The machine no longer sets the pace of work. The *chief* role becomes more important. He adds some coordination levels on the production's stakeholders and set the pace of work to the entire production. The *line manager* should pay attention on some issues regarding the automation:
  - Evaluate the potential of automation in its production line

- Review and optimize the resources usage
- Rethinking of the objectives and methods

Since the industrial revolution, automation ideas circulate among business leaders:

- Automation is within reach of the only companies with significant financial resources and whose production runs are exceptionally long.
- The *oil refinery* or other processing industry raw material represents the perfect operations automation example. Such companies have minimized the human intervention level near to zero. Eventually, company management could be very tight in the manufacturing operations or processing by only adding staff in charge of controls.
- The main automation advantage is to save labor but not by necessarily reducing staff, but preferably by moving it. For example, the computers' introduction in companies in the United States has grown massively the administrative staff, while the number of operators has remained stable between 1920 and 1950.

- Automation requires entrepreneurs learning to use new tools to solve new problems. The idea of getting more information is obviously likely to demoralize the director whose office is already full of reports that he has not had time to assimilate, or, more often, to read it simply.
- The real goal is to get a more streamlined operation and a more effective control without restricting the economies of labor achievement.
- Automation is a highly technical hand of the few technicians' case. Automation really bears fruit only if we learn to consider it from an entirely different angle. It is not by mechanizing or rationalizing existing methods that the best results will be obtained. Consent to rethink all the problems facing the company according to the purpose and the product becomes imperative. Finally, far from the technology field, these are questions of methods, organization, and psychology.

The conditions for the automation implementation in the company depend on economic ones. In a growth period, we observe that:

- Individuals naturally go to companies offering higher wages and grant benefits achieved through automation.

- Products manufactured in an automated business put pressure on prices with the consequent customers' loss for companies less well equipped.

The productivity gains from automation should consider investing in its infrastructure in addition to the organization migration cost to its final position.

As mentioned earlier, automation does not necessarily reduce labor workforce in enterprise. According to Diebold, the automation interest might finally be getting a lot more efficiency in the daily management instead of the quest for saving labor.

The risk to multiply or perpetuate inefficiency on early operations during the automation implementation remains significant. Therefore, in reality, the main automation goal is not necessarily to go faster, but to do better.

This study concluded that *a fully automated plant remains a myth*. Any manufacturing process, handling, and assembly of parts show perfect only if periodic human interventions are held to correct the defects.

Systems and systems thinking

In the early twentieth century, the reductionist-mechanistic idea inherited from the

Scientific Revolution philosophers [19] dominates thinking: all phenomena occurring in the Universe can and should be explained by the physical laws of motion. The implementation of the Taylorism and Fordism theories within enterprises represent a clear application of the Cartesian approach that drives the mechanist idea of the work.

A new way of thinking has emerged in trying to add to the Cartesian thinking some parameters that take in account the human subjectivity stemming from arts and various spiritual traditions. That combination has produced the *systems thinking*. For the latter, the system becomes the reference and cannot be reduced only to the sum of its components. In other words, the sum of its components is not sufficient to explain the whole, which is the system itself on the contrary of the Cartesian thought.

This new approach of the reality's perception can be explained in large part by the increasing complexity of the economic phenomena, sociological with changing lifestyles, globalization and the interactions proliferation between these phenomena in recent decades. The reasoning of the systems thinking involves quantities of elements in motion and not on a fixed set. Apprehension of the system requires

---

[19] Among these philosophers: Descartes, Bacon, and Newton.

understanding of its consistency and its persistence over time. In such a context, the organizational chart representation is not enough to explain the enterprise's complexity and its reality.

System combines elements, which interact with each other according to some predefined rules or principles. The system is qualified by the nature of its components and their interaction is clearly defined within its environment. Several principles depict the system:

- A system contains elements associated in some way with each other
- A system eventually overlaps another system
- A system is optionally superimposed on another system
- A system has a lifetime
- The space limits the system's scope
- A system has the possibility to exchange with its environment through inputs and outputs at large
- A system consists of processes that transform inputs into outputs

In addition, the systems' specialists consider some other axioms to integrate in that thinking:

- A system is a complex and dynamic set, which interacts as a structured functional unit

- The flows of energy, material, and information occur between its components
- A system is a community located in a predefined environment
- The flow of energy, matter, and information goes from and into the surrounding environment within semi-permeable membranes or boundaries
- The systems are often composed of entities seeking equilibrium. However, it also may encounter oscillating, chaotic, or exponential behaviors

Systems analysis appears therefore as an alternative and complementary approach to the Cartesian logic. The following table depicts a comparison between both approaches:

System	Cartesian logic	Systems logic
Knowledge	Know everything and demonstrate all the scientific analysis.	Represent a simplified view and analyze the model relevance
Understanding	Decompose, deduce and whole rebuild the whole	For the overall analysis and exchange between the system's elements.
Origins	It is always possible to go back to a cause or final causes.	It is necessary to reason from the structures. Stable relationships appear between its elements. The finalized systems work like if they had a predefined purpose.
Scope	Being exhaustive, one can understand and discover all the world secrets through a scientific endeavor.	It is not possible to take in account all the details. Simplify the phenomenon with the appropriate selection of some of its variables.

In the 1960s, the J. W. Forrester's work[20] extended the systems theory applied to business. These studies consider the company as a complex system composed of subsystems. He highlighted the characteristics of systems for analysis purposes.

The company is a concrete system, but it is also both an abstract system containing the intangibles that give

---

[20] "Principles of Systems", Jay Wright Forrester, 1968

the company its "life," like its corporate-culture concept. The company is an organization and an open system, because it creates constant relations with its environment in order to draw resources while there suffering the constraints. Constantly changing, the company may have various states. The company appears to be a completed system, addressing one or more objectives such as maximizing profit, turnover, or obtaining market share, and so forth. The company is a regulated system, which constantly adapts itself to both internal and external shocks.

With such system perspectives, the study of the enterprise complexity requires a comprehensive approach:

- Focusing more on trade between parts of the system and the analysis of each of them
- Reasoning with respect to the system purpose
- Moreover, establishing the possible stable-system states

Several policies emerge with the study of the relationship between the company and its environment:

- The production process policy, which focuses on the goods production according to the request in a reluctant changing environment.
- The inputs transformation policy, which optimizes the production technology.

- The market economy policy, which focuses on the selling of increasingly sophisticated goods in a changing environment. Selling becomes a priority to adapt the overall enterprise situation very quickly to the new market conditions.

For the systems thinking applied to the business, the company consists of three subsystems:

- The *production* system containing the goods and services production activities, especially the raw materials movement, spare parts, material resources, support systems, and automated production.
- The *information and decision* system based on the formal and informal information exchange between the various company's stakeholders, both internally and externally to the environment.
- The *strategic human resource mobilization* system leading to human action according to predefined targets.

This school of thought has allowed some big names from sociology from going further in detail in their organizational structures' research, such as Henry Mintzberg in his new approach to understand the organizational structures.

Organizational configurations

Following the initial organization definition as "how some complex elements are structured and articulated together" completed by Mintzberg's research[21], it is possible to set a new definition that takes into account the *combination of the most appropriate means to achieve its goals at best*. To setup an organizational structure within an enterprise aims to ease the flow of work or at least prevent the deformation of its current working flows. The organizational structure increases the speed of flow's execution and the overall business fluidity. The organization scheme is a mind construct or an intellectual conception on which any analyses must take into account, at least its two main aspects: structure and dynamics.

Initially, the labor division and thus the responsibilities, resources, and goals distribution involves an organizational structure definition. With the high pace of change of work conditions, new organization schemes have emerged since the industrial revolution. However, the variety of organizational structures maintains some similar structural features.

In 1979, Henry Mintzberg published the results of his research in a book entitled "The Structuring of Organizations: A Synthesis of the Research". Within

---

[21] "The Structuring of Organizations", Henry Mintzberg, 1979

his book, he describes a *generic* organization structure representation based on five components:

- The *strategic apex* corresponding to the top management of the company from which emerges the highest level of decision.
- The *middle line* consists of middle managers in charge to animate the working teams.
- The *operating core* forms the operational basis of the company, which gathers all the directly productive work.
- The *technostructure* composed of analysts and experts who work indirectly on productive activities.
- The *support staff* involving in various supports ensuring proper operation of all units.

Under the systems-thinking approach, Mintzberg adds an intangible component that connects all of its structure's elements with its environment: the *ideology*. The latter is like a halo of beliefs, values, norms, and traditions.

Every organization needs to coordinate its efforts to achieve its goals. According to the above-described model, there are six coordination forms:

- *Mutual adjustment* in one embodiment of a work subject to informal communication, usually given orally to coordinate.

- *Direct supervision* with one person that issues orders and work instructions to several other individuals.
- *Standardization of work* processes with the formal specification generally following the technostructure's work processes.
- *Standardization of outputs* with the formal outcome specification usually done by the members of the technostructure.
- *Standardization of skills and knowledge* standardizes the coordination of the work achieved through specific performers' training.
- *Standardization of norms* where an overall policy controls the work and usually is set for the entire organization. Everyone works accordingly to the same foundation of beliefs.

Some organizational structures may appear by varying the generic organizational configuration components size. In reality, Mintzberg's research highlights five main configurations:

- The *simple* or *entrepreneurial* structure is characterized by a short stature where the contractor occupies a central position. That structure is relatively informal, which allows her to react quickly to changes and perturbations. She usually does not resort to a technostructure or to a dedicated logistical support. In addition, the line is very close to the top, which is rarely expanded, and she leaves a limited space for the definition of many hierarchy levels. Slight standardization allows this structure to adjust itself quickly.

- The *machine bureaucracy* operates in a stable environment implemented with a standardized and routine work. This setup has the five components with highly formalized activities.
- The *professional bureaucracy* operates in a stable environment, but often complex and within decentralized organizational form. She leaves a maximum of autonomy to its employees. The strategic summit merely provides guidelines for action. The support function, which is highly developed, ensures the coordination between the operational teams' members.
- The *divisionalized* form is needed when the company size has to expand the market shares and requires the achievement of economies of scale. Divisions may be done according to a product structure, product line, country, and so forth. Each division, which is built from an elementary structure, keeps some level of autonomy. However, each division is still headed by a branch that sets strategic

objectives. The support functions are critical because they ensure coordination between divisions. Each division manager applies the selected breech strategic guidelines and reports the results.
- The *adhocracy* or *innovative* structure works on complex and dynamic environments. This structure is particularly adapted to a changing environment. It highlights innovation by an information exchange between the horizontal technostructure's experts and support. Autonomy is strong and is justified by the high members' qualification. The operational base does not appear: there are no "performers" in Mintzberg's definition of structures.

Thereafter, Mintzberg added two new configurations:

- The *missionary* organization with a very informal structure and operation based on a common ideology.
- The *politicized* organization without specific hierarchy where everyone is trying to impose its point of view by using its power. The decision-making results from the political games.

As the divisionalized shape definition, the organization may contain other configuration *substructures*.

Detailed analysis of the generic organizational structure representation reveals some contradictory forces even with divergent objectives:

- The strategic summit aims to strengthen the centralization with coordination by direct supervision.
- The technostructure wants to coordinate by standardizing work processes and considers the organization as a machine bureaucracy.
- The operational core's members specialize and want to coordinate the organization through standardization of skills to develop their independence in order to drive the overall structure to a professional bureaucracy.
- Intermediate hierarchy levels want to keep their power, their distance from their subordinates, and their autonomy in managing their units. This will force the organization to become a divisionalized structure.
- The support staff's members should work with other members of the structure's elements, pulling the structure to an adhocracy.

Two of these configurations use the term "bureaucracy" which leads to impart a pejorative sense for many individuals. Indeed, bureaucracy usually means excessive influence or public administration power, characterized by its slowness, its heaviness, its lack of flexibility or inability to deal with individual cases. Therefore, that definition reveals a great importance within an enabling environment for the automation implementation or optimizing administrative-tasks handlings. Let's go back to the initial definition of bureaucracy within the latest century.

Bureaucracy

Laws and regulations govern the Weberian bureaucracy (1921) organization where several principles drive its operations:

- The authority subjects individuals only as part of their official duties
- A clearly defined jobs hierarchy, which divides responsibilities between individuals
- Each job has a clearly defined competence sphere
- The labor contract sets the employment scope
- The recruitment is based on the employee's skills (qualifications and / or experience)
- The hierarchical grade-level fixes the employee's salary
- The incumbent has and is giving his entire attention to his job
- The logic determines career promotion with respect to the years of service and superiors' appreciation

- People do not own their production tools
- Individuals undergo a strict and systematic control in their work

According to Weber[22], the whole organization needs to be bureaucratic based on written and finalized rules. The skills must regulate the levels of authority within the enterprise. The labor division thus proceeds of the authority gained by the expertise and knowledge.

The adapting difficulties affect the whole enterprise and the inability to deal with specific undefined cases appear with the application of the strict and excessive detailed formalization of the organization's activities. That formalization ultimately meets the pejorative definition of the bureaucracy.

Machine bureaucracy

Henry Mintzberg describes two bureaucracies' forms: *machine* and *professional*. This first category puts the standardization of processes at the heart of its operations, which reveals some characteristics:

- Highly specialized tasks
- The routine operational tasks
- Very formalized procedures
- A centralized decision-making authority

---

[22] "Max Webers Theory of Bureaucracy and Its Negative Consequences", Felix Merz, 2013

- The usage of resources planning systems
- An administrative structure developed

Unlike the Weberian bureaucracy, the machine bureaucracy does not fit the skill key to the organization operation, but more on the operations standardization.

Professional bureaucracy

The professional bureaucracy bases its operations on skills standardization. With a limited hierarchy and a key summit with limited powers, it has an operational base with a high competence level to dispense with any formalization. With this high competence level, professionals have considerable autonomy and hold substantial power in their work realization. In this configuration, unlike the machine bureaucracy, competence is central to the functioning and can respond to unplanned events. Tasks can be repetitive but sometimes require complex intellectual reflection in order to complete.

Contingency factors

The choice of the organizational configuration depends on its pursued objectives. However, that choice following Mintzberg's thinking is also influenced by a set of criteria or contingency factors:

- The *age* of the enterprise and its ability to evolve and maintain its life and revenues over the time. The formalism is directly proportional to the enterprise seniority. The business processes become monotonous and the way they operate and the employees' skills freeze with the passing of time.
- The *size* of an organization in terms of its employees' number. An organization that employees many individuals request a dedicated structure to address particular problems to coordinate the whole set in line with the objectives.
- The more or less sophisticated *technical system* determines the support levels thereof and the method of organization operation.
- The centralized or decentralized relations of *power* within the structure that defines its hierarchy of delegation.
- The simple[23] or complex *environment*, which directly influences the structure and the way of organizing its running. The environment may be stable or dynamic, which influences the organization as illustrated in the table below.

---

[23] The environment is seen as simple if an individual has the ability to know every detail to it; otherwise, that environment should be seen as a complex one.

Environment	Stable	Dynamic
Simple	Machine Bureaucracy. Business process standardization	Simple structure
Complex	Professional Bureaucracy	Adhocracy

The contingency school includes several works of many authors, in which we distinguish two theories of contingency: strategic and structural. For the strategic one, the structural contingency theory pays too importance on the influence of the environment on the organization structure. On the contrary, the supporters of the strategic contingency theory preferably think that the managers who contribute with their decisions to the setup of the organizational structure.

Technology and organization

In 1957, Joan Woodward publishes the result of her research about the relationship between the technology and the organizational structure [24]. These results attempt to demonstrate several aspects:

- There is no significant relationship between technology and the total organization size
- Neither its size, nor its history, nor its business branch explains the performance difference of the organization
- The technology choice seems to explain the performance differences
- Technology influences the organizational structure
- The recourse of a similar technology between two organizations leads to a similar organizational formatting
- The hierarchical levels increases the complexity of the implemented technology

According to Woodward, the organizations diversity that explains the company performance highlights the lack of comparable effectiveness between various technologies employed. The technology implementation and production mode determine in this

---

[24] "Industrial Organization: Theory and Practice", Joan Woodward, 1965
"Management and technology (Problems of progress in industry)", Joan Woodward, 1966

case the company prosperity. This principle challenges the Taylor's position "one best way" with the sole task sequencing as the origin of its performance.

Woodward has also established a list of many production modes:

- The *unit* production or small batch production is achieved only after a confirmed order and is specific to each customer.
- The *mass* production produces a result in a linear assembly made up of several positions to its final form mode. This form corresponds to the Fordism application in the company with the economies of scale as a primary objective on the standardized scores production. Its implementation requests a long term and tends to limit the ability to meet customer needs while providing large stocks of goods. In general, if the production line encounters some problems, it will not be stopped.
- The *continuous* production, which processes materials continuously, operates like the chemical industry. Generally, this form reflects significant automation without any human intervention or highly reduced human intervention.

Depending on the production mode, there are various characteristics more or less marked in the organizational structure as shown in the table below:

	Unit based	Mass based	Continuous based
Number of management levels	Low	Medium	High
Supervisory span of control	Low	High	Low
Ratio of managers to total workforce	Low	Medium	High
Skill level of workers	High	Low	High
Overall Structure	Organic	Machine	Organic

The change from a unit based production into a continuous production results in increased performance and greater ease of prediction and control for the company due to increased standardization.

Mass production depicts interesting features in the context of automating tasks. Indeed, mass production corresponds to the Mintzberg's machine bureaucracy configuration. It is therefore important to note other aspects: control-wide supervision, relationship between leaders, and moderate to significant global workforce.

Variability controlled by formalizing

In the 1960s, Charles Perrow [25] studies several organizations with various sizes considering the technology as a process of transforming inputs into one or more outputs. The concept of variability refers to the number of exceptions raised during the operator's work performance. As a solution, the formalization of the work may correct that as illustrated in the table below.

	Low variability	High variability
Formalized activity	Routine activities. Formalized and centralized organization	Engineering activities. Organic and centralized organization
Low formalized activity	Crafts. Decentralized and flexible organization	Non-routine activities. innovative Organization

The activity formalization is easier in environments that depict little variability. However, it is easier if the production process is also highly standardized as well as the production outcome.

Power and control

The authority reflects the power related to hierarchical position or function. It is an established formal power recognized in the organization. The future of the company depends solely on its owners' decisions.

---

[25] "Complex Organizations: A Critical Essay", Charles Perrow, 2014

However, in large companies, things may not be so simple. Indeed, based on Mintzberg's research[26], two influence levels or stakeholders enforce organization of the power relationships:

- Individuals from the enterprise's outsiders or external organizations as members of the *External* coalition
- Individuals or organizations as members of the *Internal* coalition

The external coalition power delegates the decision-making authority to the company's CEO, who then shares it to the internal coalition's members. That delegation is accompanied by controls implementation:

- The *personal* control system by which the manager works directly with subordinates in order to control and adjust their behavior.
- The *bureaucratic* control by the introduction into the organization of directives, memoranda, and other standards to be followed by individuals. Remember, the organization's technostructure produces and formalizes these standards under the strategic apex.

---

[26] "Power in and Around Organizations", Henry Mintzberg, 1983

This second category includes three subcategories of standards imposed to the employees:

- The person's work definition or the standardization of work
- The work performance or its results
- The skills and knowledge required, defined, and standardized

More and more companies use documented procedures collections respecting general standards from the outside world. The job is then to adapt to the enterprise's business realities and describe just enough without distorting either.

Deming in his reference book on quality management advises companies to use the documentation procedures: "procedures and documents are liberators tools that relegate problems already solved in stage of routines and allow the creative faculties to be available for the remaining ones."

In addition, drafting procedures do not occur in response to a normative obligation, but strengthen the company responsiveness. Procedures help users. They make intelligible the complex relationships between the various units and company activities and their links with its environment. Thus, indirectly, their design and writing contribute to a reform of the understanding about the company in its mission and ways to accomplish the mission.

The market offers advocating standards defining procedures as the ISO9001's. The table below summarizes the standard procedures features with the quality system establishment in the company.

Procedure	Description
Mastering of Documentation	Rules adopted for documentation and retrieval systems controlled to avoid anarchic documentation management.
Mastering the quality records	Rules adopted in recording incidents that represent quality breaches.
Internal Audit	Verifying effectiveness of the quality system of rules and precautions to be aware of as many
Mastering Nonconforming products	Rules to be applied when detecting an error
Corrective action	Responding in the presence of an adverse event that requires a consultation for resolution
Preventive action	Evaluate opportunities to respond effectively to a potential risk

Standardization work meets some behavior formalization in a formal setting. In the lack of framework, or when some difficulties arise in its implementation, the establishment of a standardized output within a control system and planning remains necessary. That system makes in advance the decisions and defines the actions' consequences on companies, which must achieve an expected outcome.

The power distribution does not necessarily come from the top of the hierarchy. Indeed, experts have power based on their competence and can shape an internal coalition to influence decisions. Other power and control forms from the ideological system can fit in organizations. In this case, they are preferably informal norms based on historical or corporate culture that support decisions. Ultimately, the control system determines the employee autonomy degree.

The control system performance ensures that the formal organization goals are quickly becoming operational. Goal setting quantitative form will be accomplished through a hierarchical structure that can easily enroll in the organizational configuration. For example, quantitative objectives determine the overall goals for the company such as growth and profit through their impact throughout the hierarchy. This objectives hierarchy also reduces the time frame to the implementation of the control system. However, the definition of a larger set of specific and operational objectives highlights some constraints and difficulties to maintain for the long-term the overall system itself.

In theory, the reach of the enterprise's formal goals depicts the realized objectives distributed among the units. Now this is not the case; the link between a goal and a behavior is not direct. The desire for action, motivation, must also be present to provide this link. The sum of the whole must produce consistency in intentions. The organization then sees itself as a system for a dedicated outcome consistently.

Organizational goals show some basic features:

- Clarity
- Consistency between the decision and delay
- Intentionality presence
- Strong Ideology

Parkinson law

After studying the British administration in 1957, Northcote Parkinson[27] presents the eponymous law: "Any work increases to entirely occupy the time devoted to him." This finding comes from research that empirical results have shown that the work expansion came from the lack of relationship between a given work and the team size in charge. With a constant workload, the team can grow without causing significant impact on the task achievement.

---

[27] "Parkinson's Law Hardcover", C. Northcote Parkinson, 1996

Two forces drive behavior specific to this expansion:

- Manager needs to multiply his subordinates, not his rivals. Then, he tends to:
    - divide the work to prevent one of his employees from challenging him
    - increase coordination needs internally
    - increase the hiring of additional staff
    - increase the tools, the means to control, the number of reports, and finally the resources consumption ultimately to do the same initial amount of work
- Individuals will create another work by adding coordination, thus communication, tools and new measures definition, or eventually a new configuration within the organization.

According to Parkinson, his empirical formula leads to the inevitable increase employee with a six percent rate per year, regardless of the amount of work to do.

Neo-Taylorism

During the 1990s, Japanese industry has developed new production methods in response to the economic crisis. So, several strategic initiatives were introduced:

- The *just-in-time* production in response to a customer order based on the motto "the customer the king." The company adapts itself to the customer needs by following market trends and technology in order to sell them their products quickly. The outsourcing choice of several activities within small units decentralizes the production. So, the company should constantly control all the way from order to delivery through the processes' performance.

- The *quality control* based on "zero defect, zero time, zero stock" in order to match the client's needs and reduce its ease to turning to competition.
- The *traceability* with ongoing monitoring to ensure that the product matches the client's order by making workers responsible for their own production. Thus, the enterprise establishes formal procedures to monitor the production process and identify the time and the responsible worker for the error when it occurs.
- The *certification*, where the enterprise's units must be able to respond with the precise requirements definition for quality and traceability methods according to the established standards and be constantly monitored. Indeed, that initiative corresponds

to the standardization of the process as described by Mintzberg's theory.

These initiatives' implementation actually improve the quality of production. However, some other consequences appear:

- The need to maintain a mass-production process while developing individualized and customized products.
- The stress increases due to the just-in-time production. The line must run at all cost and without any mistakes. The associated control systems to that production line directly highlight the responsibilities of faulty operation. This adds also a certain amount of stress to the workers.
- The global view replaces the business logic.
- The leader no longer sets the pace of work of the worker, but the customer does. More than half of the employees believe that external demand requires an immediate response.

Certification requires the company to control every production system phase. For this, a specification formula for all the workers' movements or the working methods that each employee must meet in order to obtain or retain its quality label. The quest for market differentiation in a competitive market generally justifies this approach to increase the brand value to consumers. Competition, including international, becomes more and more the quality requirements for the company. The company needs to develop a more-effective and qualitatively flawless production system. The labor exploitation under the pretext of seeking the respect of quality standards reintroduced Taylor's values in the organization. The quality objective requires minimization of defects and malfunctions that an only rigid system can provide and then, some consequences appear:

- Reduces the autonomy of workers
- Adds more normed control and administrative processes
- Increases the cost of the production.

Theses consequences show us that the quest for quality requires the maintenance of a balance between quality and cost generated by the standardization of the company's activities.

Energy and organization

The organization is a system: it consumes resources to achieve its goals such as survival and growth. Resource consumption is the necessary energy that ensures both the production of the expected outcomes and the maintenance activities. In an intangible production, that second destination would correspond to the charge of administrative tasks indirectly bringing the value in the product or customer service. However, this finding is partially correct. The additional energy consumption in the coordination of all ensures the smooth running of the production without satisfying the energy consumed during production and its support. That energy used for the coordination is not found within the delivered product or service and the customers generally ignore it. The latter is often reluctant to put the price for it, because that consumption is not justified from its point of view. Thus, the energy[28] is well distributed among all parts of the system.

In physics, *entropy* corresponds to the transformed energy into heat. It is characterized by the irreversible destruction of part of the energy required for the correct system operation and it measures the system's disorder state. This heat energy loss also contributes itself to increasing its global disorder. A high system's entropy reduces its elements' links and coordination. This affects the system's ability to produce mechanical effects and increase the share of energy unusable in the work performance. In a completely closed system, that phenomenon is growing.

---

[28] "A Student's Guide to Entropy", Don S. Lemons, 2013
"Non-equilibrium Thermodynamics and the Production of Entropy: Life, Earth, and Beyond (Understanding Complex Systems)", Axel Kleidon, Ralph D. Lorenz, 2004

Applied to the organization composed by many systems, entropy corresponds to the energy leading to anomie and thus social disorder by disintegration of the cohesive forces. The distance between the ends and means stretches: the goals away increasingly retaining means and initial resources.

Entropy also expresses the fact that everything tends to deteriorate over time. Therefore, any optimization that solves a problem today obviously becomes a problem in the future.

The optimization will be done by reducing the entropy and strengthening the cohesion around organizational goals and means to achieve them. The *negative entropy* is an organization of systems factors opposing the natural tendency toward entropy. This principle cannot be applied to pure physics, because the system produces more energy than it consumes to maintain itself. This leads to an open system. In this case, if we compare this account to the living, nature works through material or energy imports taken from its environment. This material is a free energy carrier considered as negative entropy. The open systems theory[29] is the foundation of a *neguentropic* trend of body systems, "the body feeds on negative entropy" and thus reduces the entropy, or delays the degradation

---

[29] "General System Theory: Foundations, Development, Applications", Ludwig Von Bertalanffy, 1969

of the system. Similarly, the optimized organization draws its energy from its human resources through its maintenance of a strong cohesion.

The organization life cycle

In biology, all living beings follow a life cycle with at least four steps:

- Birth
- Growth
- Maturity
- Decline

Each system[30] that makes up the company will take its own life cycle but with contingencies between them. Indeed, proper operation of the business is characterized by the alignment of sales system with the development of the product and the production system. Otherwise, this nonalignment will be a recovery in advance of any automation.

From a global perspective, the company has its own life cycle:

- The enterprise's *birth* characterized by a simple organizational structure where the activities are rarely formalized. That structure

---

[30] Production, R & D, information, policy, hierarchical, etc.

remains very flexible and easily adaptable to its environment demands.
- The *growing* period with increasing volumes of activities and complexity. It is therefore necessary for the entrepreneur to delegate authority. That coordination scheme takes the form of direct supervision.
- The *maturity* period with the objective to maintain its activity and profit level by putting pressure on costs. The configuration is also driven toward the setup of divisions, machine or professional bureaucracy.
- The *restructuring* period within a significant competition. The company begins to anticipate the need for change, because the reduction of costs is not enough to reverse the declining profits trend.
- The *decline* marked by a significant reduction of the activity volume accompanied by a drop in sales and the continued rise in costs. Without any adequate responses, this decline led to the end of the business.

Unlike biological beings, the company can still react during his decline and will bring new energy, innovate, and start a new life cycle. This reactivity depends on some of the defined earlier contingency factors: age, environment, technology.

Organizational silos

The organization refers to the concept of *silo* reused from the agricultural world as a form of some activities' separation made deliberately opaque to the rest of the organization's members. However, be careful to consider the organizational silos as necessarily detrimental to the proper company functioning. For example, in a professional bureaucracy configuration like this could be justified by the rally in the same unit of highly skilled managers of complex activities, from which only the result counts for the rest of the organization skills. However, in most cases, silos represent situations even more important when locking members intervene on transverse processes.

Several observations [31] can identify the presence of silos:

- The only way to get something from the silo's members is exclusively from its hierarchical top, very rarely at the bottom, and still less by the middle hierarchy. The silo's head tries to attract talented profiles for their professional capacities and not necessarily for their management skills.

---

[31] "Lost in management : La vie quotidienne des entreprises au XXIe siècle", François Dupuy, 2011

- The silo's head leads the silo and has all the authority and reign over his silo. He is the only one who decides. He is very active in politics and spent much of his time to prove to the others his existence and usefulness to the entire company.
- The silo has its own procedures and management tools. The main enterprise's technostructure does not have access to them or access is very difficult and cannot intervene directly in a comprehensive approach. The need to improve the existing situation will be under the sponsor of the line manager and the improvement will affect only the structure's elements.
- In case of organization change or resources' reallocation, the silo's members prefer that it will happen to others.
- The silo has created its own technostructure and logistical support independently of the main enterprise's technostructure and support.
- Silo's members do not know, and often do not want to know, what is happening outside their silo, that is to say in the rest of the organization.
- The silo has the ability to create easily barriers to collaboration with the rest of the organization.

- Many hierarchy levels and committees where the decision-making is finally dissolved.

The organizational silo is created following a combination of opportunities and circumstances to which the Parkinson principles find a fertile ground to growth. Starting from a *simple* structure composed with the basic elements, a change occurs and triggers the movement. Mister *Y* previously integrated into the organization receives the authority or developing his own authority sidelines of his current organization. Then justifying application for his environment, he is extracted from the group to create his own branch. He is the first one to break free the activity. He then begins to attract operational profiles while away from the land, the operational part. He now needs to control his team. He is jointly developing the tools for planning and control, as he needs information from his own silo. Project accumulation requires its technostructure or a dedicated support setup. With time, the head, Mister Y, is moving away from his operational base by creating new authority lines with a new functional division within the view "divide and reign." So, Mister Y is spending more and more energy to maintain the same job with more coordination, more control, more reports, and so forth. To justify the investment front, Mister Y will not hesitate to diversify and find elements of growth directly outside the organization if necessary. As a cost center, he tries to become a profit center without consulting the rest of the organization. Mister Y ultimately divides the organization. In such an organization, this could happen again with Mister X, Mister Z, and so on.

The silo usually has its own tools and communication with the outside of the organization is often done in a non-formalized manner through e-mails or the exchange of physical documents.

The transverse business processes execution that involved silo's members displays some dysfunctions:

- Several input of the same information
- Informal information exchange from the hierarchical top
- Lack of accountability on the transverse process with the distribution thereof among several departments making improvements to the relatively complex process

Therefore, in the process optimization classroom, we often heard the way to "breaking silos" in order to improve the whole enterprise's efficiency. True, however, that goal is difficult to achieve, as the energy initially deployed to create the silo is so significant. Suppressing a silo will require a proportionally greater energy to develop than that used in its design time. In the absence of an external coalition, the solution will favor the "drill a hole" in the silo approach by promoting exchanges without changing the structure in integration logic. This solution focuses on the respect and appreciation of the structure while creating opportunities to leverage talent within organizations. Those organizations within the enterprise solutions can consider maintaining competitiveness and growth without neglecting the required effort.

Outsourcing

Before globalization and changes in information technology, more and more companies are inclined to shift more or less an important part of their business internationally through the following objectives:

- Check and reduce operational costs; that is to say, achieve better control over the external costs evolution in relation to the internal company costs development. Initially seen as a fixed-costs generator, the business activity produces therefore variable costs directly related to the production level or the trading activity volume.
- Increase competitiveness by refocusing activities on the company's core business. This refocusing is performing in relation to its goals and ideology on the one hand and, on the other hand, taking advantage of outsourcing human and physical skills that are not hers on other trades.

- Provide flexibility and responsiveness to be able to adapt quickly to the market changes.

The outsourcing mainly affects businesses deemed non-core and typically located in the functions of little logistical support generating revenue. However, in some cases, the company did not hesitate to restructure and outsource a substantial part of its generating revenue core business.

The literature on this subject distinguishes *outsourcing* from *subcontracting*. With outsourcing, the transferring company continues to monitor the activities through a past with the executing company, albeit with the possibility of reversal formal agreement under conditions.

Unsurprisingly the activities that are mainly outsourced are the most formalized within the company, or the activities that largely produces standardized outcomes. Indeed, little formalized, complex, or generating profit for the company tasks are rarely outsourced, while transferring formalized business processes to others is easier.

In general, outsourcing affects fewer departments pursuing the commercial activity of the company managing the IT infrastructure. However, if the outsourcing of few formalized activities is chosen, those activities will be at least formalized and detailed in order to fulfill the contract terms and conditions set between the entities.

By outsourcing some of the activities, several cross-business processes can be split. The firm boundary redefinition introduces a new customer-supplier relationship. Outsourced processes become services with levels determined in advance. The legal constraints introduction in service delivery reduces its flexibility. What once was not static and subject to debate then becomes a potential conflict source when the requested accommodation is beyond the scope originally intended. Outsourcing promotes the new skills or new functions development in the company, related in particular to control the supplied service levels.

Outsourcing also has some disadvantages:

- Loss of control and skills of the outsourced functions, especially over time and if the claimant must serve many clients because of similar benefits.
- The decline in quality following the lack of predefined quality level.
- The dependence with the service provider.
- Lack of transparency because the company outsourcing finds it impossible to verify the occurrence of spirals of subcontracting

incurred by the service provider subject to the same constraints of staffing restrictions and competitiveness. It comes back on Taylor's approach, not on individuals but on businesses and uncontrollably. The production company is an assembly of components from companies. This may simply result in the formation of social crimes, loans labor and illicit deals.
- Fear of outsourced activities' irreversibility and the inability to go back and have to recreate these activities in-house if necessary.
- The impact on human resources, corporate culture, and work collectives, measuring changes that outsourcing leads to the transferred employees and fears for the future for those who remain. Negative reactions occur with internal conflicts, decreased productivity, or more insidiously individual and collective confidence loss. When outsourcing also means a positions transfer, the operators concerned must adapt to new working conditions. The sense of belonging becomes less important to the company and its team projects outsourced versus in-house team. Note also increasing employment volatility due to the activity transfer.

Outsourcing affects how various stakeholders work organization and coordination. As Taylorism, cutting activities demand reinforcement in the control and coordination of all without having sufficient power and constrained by contractual clauses. The reflection of outsourcing will result in the company outsourcing a growing of many administrative tasks. This effort materializes additional costs, which have to be deducted from the outsourcing gains.

Outsourcing brings an extra dimension to the automation issue in business. The success of this initiative will depend on several criteria such as the initial knowledge of business and administrative processes, and the importance given to the staff working conditions, technical environment, and production tools.

Part III
Business Process Automation

Automate business processes

Automate business processes in heavy industry has been a common practice for years while the industrialization of an immaterial production seems to face additional difficulties. The materiality characteristic of the industrial sector plays a significant role as a key success factor for automation. As a reminder, the idealized industrial company may have the following characteristics:

- A task distribution among the enterprise's units based on the various components that form the final product
- A production according to the steps of forming and assembly of the final product in a Cartesian logic
- A mass production of standardized products
- A line work that minimizes the human intervention
- A purely mechanistic logic applied to production and based on cause-effect relationship
- An established performance management with the control of the costs issuance and their variations
- An implementation of the quality approach with a systematic improvement measurement
- A production with no waste and its defects reduced at a minimum level

- A clear and precise separation between the production's activities, support and management
- An organizational structure having few hierarchical levels, at least in the production line
- A coordination mode based on the processes standardization
- The company has some administrative and related activities externalized
- The company has some parts or components provided by third parties

The process management's activities and continuous improvement is not new to manufacturing companies, although it has a different name. As an immaterial production, reducing costs, increasing revenues and improving quality represent the main management objectives.

Third sector organizations add more nuanced characteristics to the industrials ones:

- The document in any form whatsoever represents the only tangible medium of an immaterial goods and services production. It physically denotes the link between the enterprise and the client.

- Only the information represents the treated material through the process.
- There is a blurred separation between administrative and production tasks. However, most operators perform both activities together with a distribution higher or lower depending on its unit.
- There are many workstations and computerization with many applications made available to the user.
- There is at least a centralized information system containing the key information and rules to apply to the treatment of income-generating information.
- Several satellites software applications supplement the basic information used to support or administrative duties systems.
- A complex organizational structure composed of several divisions or units.
- Coordination mode is based on methods that combine mutual adjustment and formal exchange.
- The significant decisions are made from a major responsibilities division with the appearance of a committee.

As mentioned in the second part of this book, these characteristics come with more or less importance depending on the contingency factors such as age, size, or technical systems and staff.

Most companies are running business processes without undertaking a specific approach to business process management. They make extensive use of information technology and automation in the first primary form as described in the first part of this book. The need to move to a higher-level-based automation with the BPMS introduction usually occurs following organizational problems or technical malfunctions. Noncompliant practices or simply the need to become more responsive to new fixed objectives completes that initiative goal. These companies realize the need of the various stakeholders' alignment in the process. Like earlier industrial companies like Ford, they understand that improving their performance depends on the information flows within the company. The users' workstations are optimized and specialized according to Taylor's approach. However, the following effects occur against the company performance:

- While heterogeneous information systems grow, the actual production performance requests many manual entries of the same information from different company's departments. The risk of introducing errors within the systems increase with that way of working.

- With an increase of information distribution channels, some information may be used several times in some contexts.
- An increasing number of information sources.
- An increasing number of electronic documents. This introduces difficulties storing and managing many versions, eventually introducing errors in documents.
- A randomized orders status control.
- Email represents the only communication support used for formal exchanges.
- A labor division following the logic of the stack: first in, first out. This is done without taking in account the production delays and priorities.

Like the manufacturing companies, the sentence *fluidizes the flows* in an immaterial production means the introduction on a system, which ensures:

- The control of information input with the single information entry. The introduced information is used once and available everywhere.
- The control flow and real-time measurement of the various states of information.
- The control of the documents flows.
- The control of changes.

- The control of formal information exchange between business stakeholders.

In such context, the immaterial production enterprise has several choices to implement a BPMS in its production:

- First, the simplest level would be the development of a new IT solution based on few BPMS's functionality without BPM approach integration in the enterprise. In this case, the company considers the BPMS as another computer tool added to the existing enterprise IT architecture. For the user, that solution looks like an application to manage a new business element or to replace a set of obsolete software. The BPMS plays, in this case, a role for integrating existing system solutions and avoids any duplicate data entry by centralizing some information processing. This canning implements the business processes execution and organizational structure. This new program availability limits automation tasks to a single workstation.
- The second level completes the first one by adding the information exchange between some stakeholders to produce a shared application. In this case, the BPMS provides a means of communication between one or more

users in a context very narrowly and on a particular topic. This integration does not affect the whole process since the intervention is located only in one place within the process. On such a level, the BPM's logic is not critical, since its main goal is to correct or improve a workstation.
- The third choice recourses to the BPMS workflow functionality applied directly to business information. This results in algorithmic information processing with status changes requiring the predetermined, possibly human validation. This choice centralizes the information flow processing but not the work and tasks allocation or processing.
- The most advanced level implements all the BPMS features. In this case, it does not only support the business process information flow but also the work distribution among the operators, activity reports generation and transmission, real-time monitoring, and existing systems integration, as discussed in the first part of this book.

Depending on the pursued objectives, the BPMS implementation scope may change and be applied either on the overall business process or only on some of its parts. The company plans possibly to assess the

BPMS integration in its operation following a rising trend of implementation:

- Automate administrative tasks that do not influence the processes generating the company income.
- Automate the businesses with low impact on the underlying business process returns.
- Automate the essential business processes, including customers' orders through the production of goods and services over several departments.
- Automate the business processes that incorporate directly the involved customer, which has the ability to alter its performance.
- Automate the business processes partly externalized with some partner companies to create just-in-time sub-processes. The scope includes external systems with the need to add significantly corporate governance.

To meet the most advanced form of integration, automation must be integrated into a management-approach BPM that goes beyond the IT framework. French's Larousse dictionary's entry for the definition of automation describes this critical aspect to the success of such a project:

"The automation is not simply a replacement of humans by robots, but to rethink more or less deeply the designated process and to question the acquired habits and traditional solutions. Supporting all or part of the intellectual functions involved in operating a process, the automation is located at a higher level than a simple mechanization. Integrated to the design and management of large industrial, administrative and business, automation is a key factor of increasing productivity and quality".

BPMS implementation

The enterprise's BPMS implementation initiative requires two main phases:

- The BPMS integration project within the companies that setup the system and its organization from requirements and needs analysis to its deployment.
- The daily operation integrated to the BPMS environment.

Several important issues must be added to the traditional project's management prerequisites to drive that implementation:

- Initially determine the level of the BPMS usage in the business, from a simple computer application until the usage of all of its features.

- Initially determine the automation scope, from administrative processes to the customers and partners integration processes.
- Determine the automation project context. This project is either included in a holistic approach to manage and improve business processes or an isolated improvement initiative of a particular situation. As a reminder, in the case of the BPM approach, this initiative led to the business development lifecycle in which the BPMS registers as a means of implementing improvements in addition to resolutions organizational process tracks.
- Determine the executing automated process environment and existing systems integration.
- From a systemic point of view, align or realign the various systems that make up the company. To recall, the company consists of many systems. The BPMS introduction induces inevitably variations on existing systems.

These points represent some significant criteria in order to define the budget, the criticality level, and the deadlines of that automation project.

The analysis and improvement of the current situation is done with:

- The description of its *static* or organizational structure of the organization materialized by some documents, information, or existing systems.
- The description of its *dynamic* or activities' flows, information exchange, or types of work coordination based on the organization experiences.

The environment and especially the organizational structure determine a more or less favorable environment for the BPMS implementation. For example, machine bureaucracy has some features that facilitate the business processes automation:

- A large number of employees and size of interaction.
- Some tasks largely standardized with potentially complex treatments.
- A company having its technostructure, which formalizes the operational procedures and memos respecting any external standards to the organization.
- An immaterial production based on information including computer records and documents.

- Other computer systems processing information inside and outside the organization.
- Blurred separation between administrative and goods and the production activities.

In such an environment, automation can handle a significant repetitive work amount and focus on transverse processes. Other configurations, such as the professional bureaucracy comprised of complex and non-standard intellectual activities limits the automation to its administrative tasks scope. For example, optimizing business processes of a commercial department managing the relationship with customers focus on reducing administrative tasks and free up time for sale, which represents the income generating activity for the company.

From the dynamic point of view, the coordination is important with the processes and outcome standardization in a lesser extent. Indeed, mutual adjustment provides some flexibility where it is necessary for the proper whole functioning. However, according to the analysis, the BPMS will replace this method by formalizing exchanges between employees.

The BPMS' choice represents an important stake for its implementation success. Its selection depends on various criteria:

- Its adequacy to fulfill the objectives of the enterprise automation project and desired features.
- Its information architecture complexity.
- The information technology team's skills and knowledge levels.
- The origin of the BPMS:
    - The BPMS is part of a solutions suite provided by a single supplier. The integration of computer systems favors other integrated solutions of the provider's portfolio.
    - Centralized business software dedicated to a specific business includes also a BPMS. In this case, the solution focuses only on this business. Adaptation and automation-related activities meet some integration difficulties.
    - A BPMS represents the unique solution of an independent systems provider. In addition to a focus on its evolution, that solution offers the advantage of an easier integration of various computer systems.
    - The *open source* BPMS developed by an international community of developers offering attractive prices

and great potential for adaptation to any existing IT systems.
- The operating cost including its license costs to operate, its information technology infrastructure costs, its implementation and maintenance costs.
- The history of the relationship between the supplier and the company focusing on acquisition.
- The consultant's advices.
- The periodically evaluation reports published by large research and consulting companies in information technology.

The exploitation of BPMS and its environment is the second phase of the process automation implementation in the company. This operation requires the establishment of a *governance* to support the BPMS integration as a new element of the technical architecture of the company. The governance is subject to various requirements[32] :

- The definition of the BPMS stakeholders' roles and responsibilities
- The management of the relationship with the supplier

---

[32] The ITIL library represents the mainly used in IT management activities.

- The management of incidents and problems pays attention to the incurred errors and exceptions
- The management of changes for integrating new automated process or update existing processes
- The management of the quality and the execution of compliance tests
- The management of BPMS versions
- The managing of the release and deployment into production following business requirements and constraints of information systems
- The establishment of measures and reports

The BPMS exploitation introduces a new form of organization of software development. In general, the IT department maintains several information systems and divides logically skills following the scope of these systems. Automating processes with BPMS requires new activities and a new organization between the various stakeholders:

- The *process analyst* develops and maintains the business repository at a level of detail understandable to the business relevant stakeholders. The following lists among other elements of the internal and external organizational structure, activity streams,

indicators of measures, documents and systems used. He participates in the approach to process management and responsibility extends some stages as proposed in the first part of this book.
- The *business analyst* resumes business processes to automate and is full of detailed information on the structure of data, documents, user interfaces, systems underlying sources, and distribution channels. He is playing as an intermediary between the business and the IT world. His process representation is conceptual and specific enough to be readily translated into executable processes.
- The *developer* transforms the conceptual processes into executable processes with user's interfaces development and existing systems integration.

However, these three steps represent actually a cycle. The process analyst focusing on process improvement has insufficient detailed knowledge of the underlying systems. IT constraints making it impossible to progress activity originally planned, the analysis should change its process model and identify potential impacts.

Currently, several BPMS solutions facilitate that life cycle by providing a modeling tool and performance from BPMN notation. This visual notation includes various graphic symbols to represent the business processes flow. The included workshop of the BPMS translates directly the models into executable code, which is understandable by the machine thereby improving the ease of making executable business modeled processes.

Consequences

As discussed in the second part of this book, the introduction of the automation in industry and the systematization of the line work have led to various consequences. Automating business processes across enterprises within its immaterial production could therefore encounter the same consequences:

- Automation improves quality and reduces production time depending on the automation level due to the manual tasks reduction. As automation, the less effective element forces the overall processes performance. Fewer controls also helps to reduce the time and cost.
- Workers show reluctances to implement automation due to the potential impact on their jobs. Such as industrialization, business process automation seeks to minimize manual intervention. The BPMS introduction causes the administrative or low value-added tasks disappearance even though the latter justified the use of dedicated resources.
- The staff movement observed from the industrial production chain to the system maintenance is just as difficult in the world of business process automation. Declined into several levels-based maintenance, IT governance widens the gap and reduces the potential for change operators. As in

industrialization, the operator sees the need to expand his or her knowledge and skills in order to master this new activity. This shows a paradox: the industrial labor division logic encourages specialization while its automation requires a work generalization for the same workers. However, the automation implementation is done solely through specialization. The robot has to perform the tedious tasks.
- The hierarchical level increases significantly from the expertise addition dedicated to maintaining the BPMS. As automation, this maintenance requires various transverse knowledge and skills.
- A new communication and collaboration between the various stakeholders in the process appears with the BPMS introduction.
- Depending on the case, the processes standardization replaces mutual adjustment that prevailed.
- Process automation facilitates silos perforation without suppressing them. Transverses execution process removes waiting times incurred normally with the expectations of managers' decisions. The BPMS also systematizes its audit trail. Some previous

- activities created from scratch disappear with their applications and become obsolete.
- The idea of free time some operators must not forget the causes and consequences of the Parkinson's law. Therefore, the business process automation aims to reduce administrative tasks and thereby the release time for operators and possibly relief resources for these activities.
- Added to automation is the need to collect and document business processes in an enterprise business process repository. The latter will depict the main source of information in driving organizational change and process.
- The transverse part of the process requires new responsibilities when the automated process is the subject of treatment for several departments.
- Automation facilitates the reading of the processes measures by replacing the applications originally dedicated for this purpose, which are often very costly in resources to maintain.
- The operator loses some of its autonomy in carrying out its activities. However, it depends on the position occupied in the business and automated business processes position.

- The operator perception of the automated process may generate additional stress when this process directly affects his job unlike administrative processes. The operator generally welcomes any initiative more readily reducing administrative tasks in contrast to other activities directly affecting his job.
- With the automation and tangible product production, the planning department of the technostructure has sufficient knowledge in the design of automates replacing manual tasks. In the automation world with an immaterial production, this information is insufficient. The information gathering directly from the operators on the fringes of the business process automation is necessary. This phase introduces the issue of obtaining information from an operator while the latter might feel threatened disappearance of part of its business.
- As in industrial automation in the extreme, reducing the operator role element of the chain, automating business processes produced similar effects. The lack of interest in the position ultimately leads to high staff rotations.
- On the budget, automation leads to the production costs reduction by producing more

units in promptly. The increased production involves mechanically reducing costs. However, the introduction of automation requires initial expenditure that increases the unit cost. As to production, unit costs end up diminishing the costs set for the rest, since this calculation is based on a restricted-period hypothesis. The variable production cost directly affects the total cost of production. Produce goods and services requires the combination of these three categories. Automation involves greater use of capital input relative to labor.

Conclusion

The industrial processes automation is transposed in the lightweight and immaterial production following the business process automation approach. The latter approach considers the information as a raw material processed throughout the process performance. For a long time, the information systems have supported the automatic processing, exchange, and storage of information. However, even if these systems support the production, this does not mean that they have entirely industrialized the production. In comparison with the industrial world, the workstation features software tools supporting the work of the operator in an *individual - computer* relationship. All individuals responsible for achieving a goal have the freedom to establish the process according to their specialties. However, the desire to bring industrialization in an immaterial production requires a higher level of automation. The relationship turns into *individual - automate - individual* within the logic of a collaboration established between individuals and information systems. The BPMS represents a solution to the establishment of that relationship by integrating the communication and integration with existing enterprise systems. However, the automation in response to the company's difficulties to align its goals and means to achieve them faces some implementation troubles. Operational underperformance of uncontrolled business processes, increasing demands for changes or adaptation of these processes to new products or services, inadequate IT solutions to business demands depict some of the reasons of the gap between the objectives and means. Over time, that gap widens and strengthens the anomie or the social degradation of the company. Automation considered as a unique means in response to close that gap would be utopian. An overall lack of consideration of the company's structure and its operations limits the scope of automation and may produce even more processes that are inefficient. In that case, the automation is often limited to a department omitting the overall view of the processes in the company. The initial performance issue is then carried over upstream and downstream of this department. So, "This is no longer my problem," some could say in such a case.

The need to automate structurally inefficient business processes therefore represents an unnecessary expense and a brake for some brand new initiative in this direction. Improving business process becomes an important step in advance of any form of automation. Similarly, the importance of the social consequences must be taken into account from the outset of any initiatives. Recall that current approaches of the process optimization in the company reflect a mechanistic approach of the organization on a basis of a rational social behavior and the recourse of simplified models. However, on the other hand, considering an "individualistic" approach like the humanistic or the systemic school, the social rational behavior trails off and the differences between the measures taken following the principles of the mechanistic approach and the individual measures appear.

From that postulate, it would be possible to be more efficient by following a coordination mode based on the mutual adjustment against the only mechanistic approach. For example, the question about how to evaluate two different sale teams running the same process but generating diverse incomes can be asked. This actually shows that thinking about automating processes must take into account the activities without seeking to reduce systematically the mutual adjustment. The contingency factors define the structure and the operation model of the organization. The automation converts units' production into mass production of a product or a highly standardized service. The set of organizational component substructures now forced execution of business processes to various transverse modes. Automation will therefore focus on the entire standardized business process, that is to say, the process whose outcome or processes are standardized by precise specifications. The comparison with the Fordism's approach therefore should be nuanced, even if the automation pursues the same objective of the partial or total removal of human intervention within the activities execution. Mutual adjustment must be maintained, even strengthened, not abolished depending on the complexity or the specific activities to be optimized. The mechanistic and systemic approach combination is used to address the key issues for the success of the automation implementation in business.

The organizational form of the machine bureaucracy would favor the automation implementation with a significant presence of a highly standardized operating model. The procedures are clearly specified and the automation would correspond to the transposition of the latters into executable tasks within the BPMS. Regarding the companies having some organizational silos, the BPMS tends to ease the information exchange and the collaboration between several stakeholders.

Considered as a system by the systemic approach, the BPMS will disrupt the existing systems once the latter is introduced in that whole. Its implementation should take into account these aspects. It has to ensure the alignment of the whole and to forge new links between all these systems. From the point of view of physics, the BPMS considered as a system undergoes its own entropy. Remember, the system will consume some of its own energy for its maintenance. The choice will be therefore driven on the BPMS offering the lowest power consumption. This idea raises the question of the cost, quality, and processing time following the introduction of the BPMS in the company. The automation implementation opportunity should be placed in relation with the cost and effort related to the initial manual execution of that activity.

The deployed energy in the BPMS goes beyond the framework of the IT infrastructure and joins the establishment of proper governance in order to lead the development of the system in the best conditions. As previously mentioned, a comprehensive approach to the process management initiative ensures the continuous improvement cycle within the company. As the automation represents a part of that cycle, the definition of change management process with its stakeholders remains necessary.

The ideal BPMS must therefore ease:

- The presentation of the information and means to the user to act directly in relation with its function
- The automation of repetitive tasks
- The monitoring of process execution with the statement and real-time measurements presentation
- The integration in a continuous improvement cycle
- The governance setup
- The existing IT systems integration
- The business processes documentation
- The communication between stakeholders in the automated processes development
- The decrease of time spent to implement the requested changes
- The decrease of the resources consumption to its implementation, both from a technical point of view and human

Measuring the performance of BPMS and its return on investment is a truly coherent issue in a long-term perspective. In the short term, it is only a BPMS cost implementation. By placing them in a comprehensive approach to quality improvement, automation seeks to produce better, cheaper, and not necessarily more quickly, especially since it gives priority to customer satisfaction. The optimization then boils down to automate business processes and business in charge of production of goods or services' standardized processes. In this case, automation allows employees to focus exclusively on tasks with high benefits and the company to differentiate itself in a highly competitive market. The company is then able to offer standardized products and services as well as other tailored products and services according to the needs of some customers.

Finally, simply recall the 1958 social automation consequences study conclusion: *a fully automated plant is a myth.*

www.ingramcontent.com/pod-product-compliance
Lightning Source LLC
Chambersburg PA
CBHW060904170526
45158CB00001B/489